HEALTH CARE ISSUES, COSTS AND ACCESS SERIES



# A HEALTH INSURANCE MODEL FOR ANALYZING LEGISLATIVE POLICY OPTIONS

# HEALTH CARE ISSUES, COSTS AND ACCESS SERIES

**The Health Care Financial Crisis: Strategies for Overcoming an "Unholy Trinity"**
*Cal Clark and Rene McEldowney (Editors)*
2001. ISBN: 1-56072-924-4

**Health Care Crisis in America**
*James B. Prince (Editor)*
2006. ISBN: 1-59454-698-4

**A New Epidemic: Harm in Health Care-How to Make Rational Decisions about Medical and Surgical Treatment**
*Aage R. Moller*
2007. ISBN: 1-60021-884-9

**Decision Making in Medicine and Health Care**
*Partricia C. Tolana (Editor)*
2008. ISBN: 1-60021-870-9

**Decision Making in Medicine and Health Care**
*Partricia C. Tolana (Editor)*
2008. ISBN: 978-1-60692-561-4 (Online Book)

**Social Sciences in Health Care and Medicine**
*Janet B. Garner and Thelma C. Christiansen (Editors)*
2008. ISBN: 978-1-60456-286-6

**Health Care Policies**
*Linda A. Bartlette and Ida F. Lawson (Editors)*
2008. ISBN: 978-1-60456-352-8

**Handbook of Stress and Burnout in Health Care**
*Jonathon R.B. Halbesleben (Editor)*
2008. ISBN: 978-1-60456-500-3

**Health Care Costs: Outlook and Options**
*Raymond W. Inhurst (Editor)*
2009. ISBN: 978-1-60692-151-7

**Medicare Payment Policies to Physicians**
*Katherine V. Bergen (Editor)*
2009. ISBN: 978-1-60692-131-4

**Comparative Effectiveness of Medical Treatments**
*Peter Villa and Sophia Brun*
2009 ISBN: 978-1-60741-109-3

**Health Care Costs: Causes, Effects and Control**
*Bernice R. Hofmann* ***(EDITOR)***
2009. ISBN: 978-1-60456-976-6

**A Guide to Public Health Research Needs**
*Raymond I. Turner*
2009. ISBN: 978-1-60692-852-3

**A Guide to Public Health Research Needs**
*Raymond I. Turner*
2009. ISBN: 978-1-60876-605-5 (Online Book)

**Handbook of Dental Care: Diagnostic, Preventative and Restorative Services**
*Jose C. Taggart* ***(EDITOR)***
2009. ISBN: 978-1-60741-281-6

**Generic Drugs: Needs and Issues**
*Ryan S. Blanton* ***(EDITOR)***
2009. ISBN: 978-1-60692-843-1

**Medicare: A Primer**
*Alice R. Williamson (Editor)*
2009. ISBN: 978-1-60741-108-6

**A Health Insurance Model for Analyzing Legislative Policy Options**
*Alan S. Burley (Editor)*
2010. ISBN: 978-1-60741-052-2

HEALTH CARE ISSUES, COSTS AND ACCESS SERIES

# A HEALTH INSURANCE MODEL FOR ANALYZING LEGISLATIVE POLICY OPTIONS

ALAN S. BURLEY
EDITOR

Nova Science Publishers, Inc.
*New York*

For permission to use material from this book please contact us:
Telephone 631-231-7269; Fax 631-231-8175
Web Site: http://www.novapublishers.com



LIBRARY OF CONGRESS CATALOGING-IN-PUBLICATION DATA

A health insurance model for analyzing legislative policy options/editor, Alan S. Burley.p. ; cm.
Includes bibliographical references and index.
ISBN 978-1-60741-052-2 (softcover)
1. Health insurance--Computer simulation. 2. Health insurance--Government policy--United States. 3. United States. Congressional Budget Office. I. Burley, Alan S.
[DNLM: 1. United States. Congressional Budget Office. 2. Insurance Coverage--economics--United States. 3. Insurance, Health--economics--United States. 4. Health Policy--economics--United States. 5. Insurance Coverage--legislation & jurisprudence--United States. 6. Models, Economic--United States. W 275 AA1 H432 2009]
HG9396.H422 2009 368.38'200113--dc22 2009031691

*Published by Nova Science Publishers, Inc. ✦ New York*

# CONTENTS

# PREFACE

Over the past several years, federal and state policymakers have considered a variety of proposals to increase health insurance coverage among the nation's residents. The federal government has devoted considerable effort, encompassing public health programs and tax incentives, to encourage U.S. residents to obtain health insurance. This book describes a model the Congressional Budget Office (CBO) developed to simulate and analyze an array of policy options involving health insurance coverage. It describes the model's design, basic methodology, and fundamental assumptions. To illustrate the model's use, this book reports estimates for two scenarios in which policy regarding health insurance coverage would differ from current law.

This is an edited, excerpted and augmented edition of a Congressional Budget Office Report, Publication Number 2719, dated October 2007.

In: A Health Insurance Model for Analyzing... ISBN: 978-1-60741-052-2
Editor: Alan S. Burley 

*Chapter 1*

# INTRODUCTION AND SUMMARY

## *Congressional Budget Office*

The federal government has devoted considerable effort, encompassing public health programs and tax incentives, to encourage U.S. residents to obtain health insurance. In 2007, the federal government will spend roughly $130 billion on subsidized health insurance provided to nonelderly low-income people through the federal–state Medicaid program and the State Children's Health Insurance Program (SCHIP). Federal tax preferences for some types of health insurance, especially employer-sponsored insurance (ESI), will total well over $200 billion.[1]

Despite the substantial efforts to promote health insurance coverage, about 44 million people under the age of 65—or just under 17 percent of the nonelderly population—will be uninsured at any given point in time in 2008. By 2017, that number is projected to be just under 50 million (absent changes in policy), or more than 18 percent of the nonelderly population, driven in part by shifts in the nation's demographics and in part by increases in average health insurance premiums. Today, about 39 percent of the nation's uninsured people are in working families whose income is between 100 percent and 250 percent of the federal poverty line. Most are not eligible for public health-financing programs, and they either are not offered, or they decline to accept, insurance through their employers. The low participation among those workers is attributable partly to their relatively low income and partly to the relatively small tax preference they receive for purchasing insurance. Because their tax rates are relatively low, the benefit of taking some compensation in a nontaxable form, like health insurance, is not as large as it is for higher-income workers.

Federal and state policymakers have considered a variety of proposals to encourage U.S. residents to obtain health insurance. Some initiatives would offer subsidies or expand tax incentives for those who purchase private insurance, some would require employers to offer coverage to their employees, some would modify existing regulations to reduce the cost of coverage for workers in small firms, and some would expand public insurance programs. It is a significant challenge to predict how various proposals would change the size of the uninsured population, influence the cost of nonpublic health insurance, or affect the federal budget.

This background paper describes the design, methodology, and basic assumptions of a simulation model developed by the Congressional Budget Office (CBO) to analyze an array of public policy options involving health insurance coverage. The model is built on characteristics of individuals that are relevant to decision making about health insurance coverage. The model gathers sets of details on income, employment, family structure, health status, premium costs, and eligibility to participate in publicly funded programs on a large sample of noninstitutionalized U.S. residents. The model's basic structure is illustrated in Figure 1.

The paper begins by describing the development of the base case—the current-law estimate of the distribution of coverage (and other relevant characteristics) in the United States in every year from 2008 to 2017. Particular attention is given to how estimates are derived for ESI premiums and for nongroup (individual) premiums for individuals in the simulation model. The individuals and families that constitute the base case are derived from recent data in the Census Bureau's Survey of Income and Program Participation (SIPP, www.sipp.census.gov/sipp/), supplemented with health expenditure data from the Medical Expenditure Panel Survey of the Agency for Healthcare Research and Quality (MEPS, www.meps.ahrq.gov/mepsweb) and with tax data compiled by the National Bureau of Economic Research (www.nber.org). The premium estimates are consistent with economic principles (insurers are expected to charge premiums that reflect anticipated health care spending for those covered by the policy as well as a loading factor that includes other costs such as administration and a risk premium). The estimates also reflect observed practices of insurers, and they conform to relevant state regulations. Additional data sources, such as the national health expenditure accounts (NHEAs), which are produced and maintained by the Office of the Actuary of the Centers for Medicare and Medicaid Services (www.cms. hhs.gov/NationalHealthExpendData/), are used to calibrate the base case data to match the best available information on current and future health care coverage and cost.

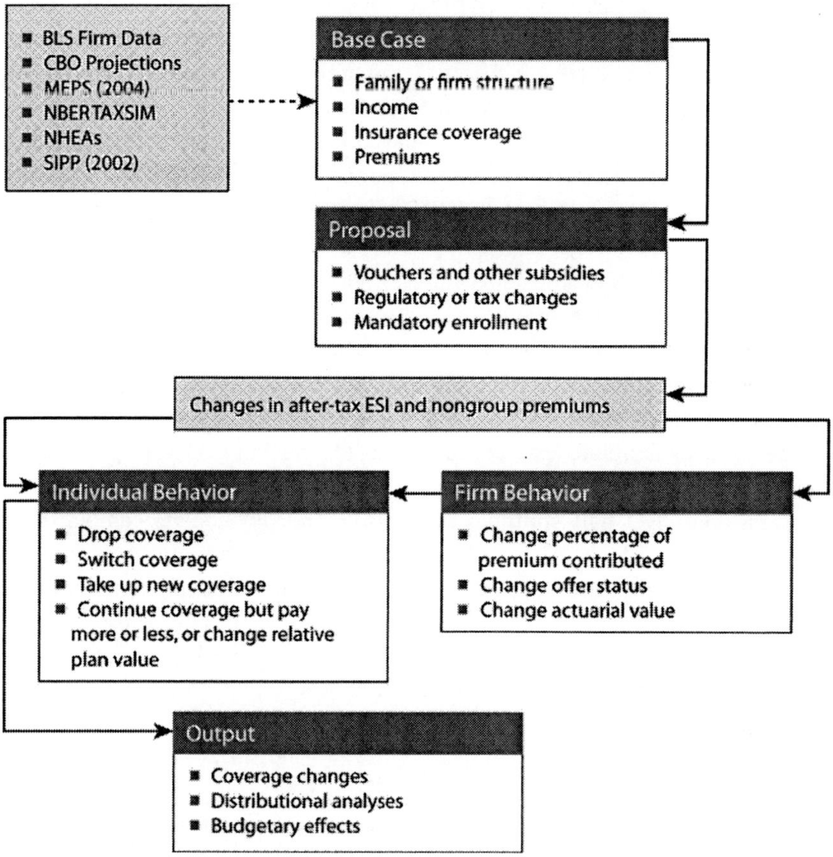


Source: Congressional Budget Office.

Notes: This diagram represents the basic flow and key components of the model. Although some elements or pathways are shown for illustration, the diagram is not meant to present every interaction or behavioral response in the model.

BLS = Bureau of Labor Statistics; MEPS = Medical Expenditure Panel Survey; NBER TAXSIM = National Bureau of Economic Research Tax Simulator; NHEAs = national health expenditure accounts; SIPP = Survey of Income and Program Participation; ESI = employer-sponsored insurance.

Figure 1. CBO's Health Insurance Simulation Model

The paper then explains the derivation and use of key parameters and assumptions that govern the main responses in the model. The first set of parameters and assumptions involve an employer's decision to offer (or decline to offer) insurance to employees based on the after-tax cost of the insurance to the firm. The next assumptions consider whether people might decide to purchase ESI (if it is offered), to purchase insurance in the nongroup market, to apply for public coverage, or to forgo health insurance. Where possible, the model's parameters are based on information in the literature, although in some cases, reasonable extrapolations and extensions were necessary; they are described in detailCBO's health insurance model is designed to analyze the effects of a host of options for expanding insurance coverage, including direct subsidies to individuals, removal or redistribution of current-law tax incentives, and insurance market reforms.

Those options can be examined for their effects on the number of insured and uninsured people, health expenditures, and distributional outcomes such as changes in insured status by age, income, and health status. The model also can be used to facilitate estimation of the federal budgetary impacts of the proposals. Although the model has many useful capabilities, it is still a work in progress, and CBO will continue to improve and develop its capabilities to provide better analysis of the types of proposals made to date and any modifications as they are developed and proposed by policymakers. Examples of two proposals recently analyzed with the model are provided in Appendixes B and C.

## End Note

[1] The most recent estimate from the Joint Committee on Taxation (JCT) for the income tax expenditure for the employer health exclusion is $109.5 billion for 2007 (www.house.gov/jct/s-307.pdf). This tax expenditure is measured as the difference between the income tax liability under current law and the liability that would result if the exclusion were repealed and taxpayers were allowed to claim the next-best tax treatment for the previously excluded employer-sponsored health insurance. That next-best treatment could be the inclusion of ESI as an itemized medical deduction on Schedule A. If that and other health-related tax deductions were repealed, the estimated tax expenditure would be considerably larger. This estimate does not include the additional loss of Federal Insurance Contributions Act (FICA) tax revenue. JCT estimates that the FICA tax exclusion for ESI will result in the loss of an additional $102.9 billion in calendar year 2007.

In: A Health Insurance Model for Analyzing... ISBN: 978-1-60741-052-2
Editor: Alan S. Burley 

*Chapter 2*

# CONSTRUCTION OF THE BASE CASE

*Congressional Budget Office*

The core data set in CBO's model is taken from the SIPP, a longitudinal survey of roughly 70,000 individuals interviewed at 4-month intervals over a 40-month period. Although the Census Bureau's Current Population Survey has a larger sample and includes an annual health insurance module, CBO relied on the SIPP in part because of its iterative design: It asks the same questions of the same respondents over an extended period. Thus, it is a better tool for modeling policy proposals that predicate eligibility on a person's having been uninsured for a specified period.

The core data on demographics, family structure, income, employment, and insurance coverage are drawn from SIPP responses covering the month of May 2002, which included a special supplement (Topical Module 5) with detailed questions about health insurance, offer and eligibility status for ESI, and health status. Those data are further supplemented with several additional questions that were presented to SIPP respondents shortly before or after May 2002. Income data are included for a full year to give an accurate measure of income and earnings. Tax-related data are taken from a previous SIPP supplement to help inform estimates of marginal tax rates. Additional data, on health status and chronic conditions, are taken from a subsequent supplement.

In: A Health Insurance Model for Analyzing... ISBN: 978-1-60741-052-2
Editor: Alan S. Burley © 2010 Nova Science Publishers, Inc.

*Chapter 3*

# HEALTH INSURANCE COVERAGE

***Congressional Budget Office***

The health insurance unit (HIU) is a key unit of analysis in CBO's model. Each HIU consists of all the members of a family who could be covered by one family health insurance policy. HIUs are created from indicators in the SIPP data that describe familial relationships of individuals in households (all individuals in a given household are surveyed in the SIPP). Three-generation families, families with children over age 22, and unmarried adults are usually grouped into separate HIUs. Only the income earned within the HIU is considered available to the unit's members, and family coverage identified within the HIU is considered as covering all HIU members and no others.

Several SIPP variables were used to ascertain the health insurance coverage status of each survey respondent. The use of SIPP indicator variables makes it relatively straightforward to determine whether a person is an ESI policyholder or a dependent. Those covered under insurance that is "privately purchased," as opposed to sponsored by a current or former employer or by a government program, were considered as having "individual market," or nongroup, coverage.

In CBO's model, SIPP survey responses indicating multiple sources of coverage are generally assumed to be accurate, and the model is designed to handle that complexity. About 3 percent of the respondents reported simultaneous enrollment in ESI and Medicaid, 1 percent reported ESI single and dependent coverage, and 1 percent reported ESI and TRICARE coverage. (TRICARE is the Department of Defense's health care program.) In some cases—for example, if it appeared that a transition from one form of coverage to another had occurred during the four-month survey period—multiple coverage was reduced to a single form of coverage.

In: A Health Insurance Model for Analyzing... ISBN: 978-1-60741-052-2
Editor: Alan S. Burley 

*Chapter 4*

# OFFERS OF EMPLOYER-SPONSORED INSURANCE

## *Congressional Budget Office*

The model identifies who is offered employer-sponsored insurance, as derived from participants' responses to SIPP questions, mostly in Topical Module 5. The SIPP survey asks workers who *are not* ESI policyholders whether health insurance is offered to any employees where they work. (Respondents who *are* ESI policyholders are assumed to have an offer of insurance even if they are not working. They could have coverage under COBRA [the Consolidated Omnibus Budget Reconciliation Act of 1985], which extends ESI after employment ends, or they could be on temporary leave.) If the answer is "yes," respondents are asked why they are not policyholders themselves. The available answers are "not eligible," "denied coverage," "chose not to be covered," and "other." Only people who give one of the final two responses are categorized as having been offered insurance.

Some researchers distinguish between people who work at nonoffering companies and those who are not eligible to enroll in the health insurance plan offered by an employer (for example, because they work part time). This distinction is not critical to the model: Incentives that might cause some employers to begin to offer insurance could just as easily cause others to extend eligibility to previously ineligible employees. If a specific policy proposal might affect the "not offered" category differently from the "offered but not eligible" category, such a distinction could be introduced into the model.

Where the responses to questions are missing or incomplete, offer status is imputed according to probability tables of offer, which are based on data from the 2004 Medical Expenditure Panel Survey Insurance Component (MEPS-IC). The probability tables are conditional on firm size, industry, uninsured status, and full- or part-time worker status.[1]

Nearly 80 percent of full-time workers are eligible for and are offered ESI in the base case, ranging from 51 percent of workers in firms with fewer than 25 employees to 88 percent of workers in firms with more than 100 employees. Overall, 71 percent of all nonelderly people (including part-time employees and nonworking people) have *access* to an ESI offer, meaning they are offered coverage themselves or they are the coverable dependents of someone who has an offer. Of the 71 percent with access to ESI, 7 percent remain uninsured; of the 29 percent of people who do not have access to ESI, 41 percent are uninsured and 48 percent have public coverage.

## End Note

[1] MEPS-IC data are based on an extensive annual survey of U.S. employers. The data were supplied to CBO by the Agency for Healthcare Research and Quality in the Department of Health and Human Services.

In: A Health Insurance Model for Analyzing... ISBN: 978-1-60741-052-2
Editor: Alan S. Burley 

*Chapter 5*

# CREATION OF SYNTHETIC FIRMS

***Congressional Budget Office***

Synthetic firms were created to model the consequences of changes in federal policy for employer-sponsored health insurance. The effect on any worker's ESI status depends in some measure on the nature of the health insurance available through that person's employer. And the insurance offering depends on the characteristics of and the demand for health insurance of the worker's fellow employees. The use of synthetic firms allows the model to more accurately reflect the fact that individual premiums depend on the characteristics of all the members of the group (because everyone is in a pool that is charged a group rate), and it acknowledges that an employer's decision to offer or decline to offer health coverage is based on the overall characteristics and preferences of the employees.

The CBO model creates a synthetic firm for each SIPP sample worker by randomly assigning as coworkers other employed SIPP respondents who work for the same size firm, live in the same region, and match the sample worker's ESI offer status. Conditional upon the SIPP worker's salary, the draw is further stratified so that the wage distribution of the synthetic firm matches that observed in data from the National Compensation Survey, which is conducted by the Bureau of Labor Statistics. As a result, the CBO model's synthetic firms reflect predominant wage patterns: A low-wage worker is more likely to be in a firm with predominantly low-wage workers, and a high-wage worker is more likely to be in a firm with predominantly high-wage workers.

One example of the usefulness of the synthetic firm is the case of a policy change that targets low-income workers, say, those whose household income falls below 200 percent of the federal poverty line. With synthetic firms, the model also can readily simulate effects on workers outside that income range who may be employed alongside workers who are eligible for the subsidy. (While federal policy may directly benefit— through a subsidy, for example— a portion of the employees of a particular firm, that firm's behavior in response to the federal policy is likely to affect more employees than just those who receive the subsidy.) The model would predict, for example, that a worker whose household income was 250 percent of the federal poverty line—and who thus would be ineligible for the subsidy—would be more likely than a higher-paid worker to be employed by a firm whose workers are eligible for the subsidy (low-wage workers are more likely to work with other low-wage workers). That worker would be more likely than someone who earns higher wages to benefit indirectly from the subsidy because the subsidy might lead the employer to offer ESI for the first time or to offer a more valuable package of benefits overall.

To simulate typical variation within firm size categories, different numbers of coworkers within each category are drawn from the sample for each SIPP respondent, based on the detailed distribution of firm sizes from the Census Bureau's 2001 Economic Census. The distribution of characteristics of a given worker's coworkers, by firm size (for example, the percentage older than 50 or the percentage in fair or poor health), closely matches survey data from the MEPS. More important, the variation in coworker characteristics is greater in small firms, consistent with what is seen in data at the firm level. A worker in a small synthetic firm is more likely than is one in a large firm to have a very high or very low proportion of coworkers in poor health.

In: A Health Insurance Model for Analyzing… ISBN: 978-1-60741-052-2
Editor: Alan S. Burley 

*Chapter 6*

# HEALTH INSURANCE PREMIUMS

***Congressional Budget Office***

All individuals in the model are assigned nongroup insurance premiums, and everyone who is employed is assigned an ESI premium. The premiums are assigned, regardless of actual coverage status, using the imputation methods described below. Generally, premiums are based on individuals' expected insurance costs, sometimes constrained by state regulations on premium ratings or other factors. In the aggregate, the cost to insurers of providing insurance coverage—including payments for health care and administrative expenses—approximately matches the premiums they charge. The processes for assigning ESI and nongroup premiums differ and are described separately below.

## PREMIUMS FOR EMPLOYER-SPONSORED INSURANCE

The ESI premium for a worker in a given firm (or for a recipient of insurance through COBRA) is based on the expected aggregate health spending of the firm's workers. The construction of ESI premiums occurs in five steps: Expected health spending is computed for each worker, that spending is averaged over all workers in the synthetic firm, a firm-specific load factor is added, the firmwide premium is adjusted to account for any applicable state regulations, and an adjustment is made that considers assumptions about the relative plan value (the value of the plan's coverage, as indicated by the size of a deductible or the amount of cost sharing, relative to other plans). The load is that portion of the premium that does not pay for health care costs. It generally includes profits and the cost of enrollment, marketing, and collecting premiums, for example. Because some administrative costs are fixed, the load tends to be a larger proportion of the premium for small businesses than for large companies.

## INDIVIDUAL-LEVEL EXPECTED HEALTH SPENDING

Individual-level expected health spending is estimated as the product of five factors:

Expected health spending = age–sex factor × health factor × experience factor × state cost factor × base

*Age–Sex Factor.* The age–sex factor is the ratio of expected spending per person within a specific age–sex group to overall expected spending per person. The factors, which were obtained from nongroup premium tables from a large private insurer (factors derived from analyses of expenditures from the MEPS as a function of age and sex are similar), are normalized so that the average factor for people who are covered by ESI is 1.0. Age–sex factors for the nonelderly range from 0.46 for children ages 2 to 17 to for 64-year-old males.

*Health Factor.* The health factor reflects expected spending based on health status, controlling for age and sex. Private insurance spending among full-year, privately insured people from the 2004 MEPS is modeled as a function of self-reported health status, controlling for age, sex, and other factors. That process yields ratios of expected spending among four health groups relative to expected spending among people with excellent health status. The ratios are roughly 1.1 (very good), 1.7 (good), 1.9 (fair), and 5.9 (poor).

*Experience Factor.* The experience factor accounts for the additional variation in expected health spending for a given year that is associated with actual spending in the year before. This factor reflects the practice of experience rating, which allows insurers to adjust ESI premiums for each firm according to that firm's claims history. The experience factors are calculated by measuring the association between spending in 2000 and 2001, after controlling for age, sex, and self-reported health status. The calculation uses the same two-year linked MEPS subsample used to construct the health factors.[1] The experience factors are centered on 1.0 and range from 0.6 for someone with little spending in the prior year to 1.9 for someone with high spending in the prior year.

*State Cost Factor.* The state cost factor reflects geographic variation in health care spending (in volume and in cost per service). Data on per capita spending for personal health care for 2000 (the most recent year available) are taken from the state health expenditures component of the NHEAs. The accounts consist of detailed national estimates of health care spending, by payer and provider categories. Those factors were adjusted to admit differences in age composition among the states, as identified from the 2000 census. The state factors range from about 0.8 to 1.2.

*Base.* The base is used to convert the rating factors into a premium in dollars. The figure is derived from total private health insurance spending from the NHEAs such that when the other factors (including loading costs) are applied, the total of all ESI premiums in the model matches total spending on private health insurance premiums in the NHEAs that is attributable to ESI.

## FIRM-LEVEL EXPECTED HEALTH SPENDING

Once expected spending is calculated for individuals, the synthetic firms are used to create expected spending factors at the firm level for single policies, based on workers' spending factors, and for family policies, based on spending factors among workers and their dependents. The firm-level spending factors are then adjusted to account for administrative and loading costs, state premium compression regulations, and relative plan value.

## LOADING COSTS

Load—the administrative, non-health-care portion of the premium—varies by firm size. Average administrative and loading costs, as a percentage of the total premium, are derived from data from the Actuarial Research

Corporation and applied according to the size of the synthetic firm.[2] Loading costs range from 9 percent of premiums for firms with 100 or more employees to 27 percent for a two-employee business.

## State Regulations

Most states regulate premium rates to limit the variation in premiums charged to small businesses. In the extreme, New York does not allow rates charged to small firms to vary on the basis of the firm's characteristics or those of its employees—the only adjustments permitted are based on location within the state. Most other states allow some degree of premium adjustment based on age, health status, or other factors. Small-firm premiums are adjusted in the model in a manner consistent with the rating regulations within the state.[3] The adjustment generally results in lowering the premiums paid by firms with the oldest and least-healthy employees and raising those of firms with the youngest and healthiest employees.

## Relative Plan Value

Premiums are multiplied by the relative plan value, which is indexed to 1.0 for an average ESI policy. In the base case, individuals are assigned relative plan values linked to an assumption (borne out by observation) that employees of large firms, people with high income, and people in poor health tend to prefer more comprehensive health insurance benefits (characterized, for example, by lower deductibles).[4] The magnitude of those adjustments is such that there is a roughly 10 percent difference between the 10th- and 90th-percentile policies ranked by relative plan value.

## Employer and Employee Contributions

Finally, the total premium is divided into employer and employee contributions, as derived from the responses to a SIPP question ESI policyholders were asked about how much they contribute to a total premium. (Non-ESI policyholders were not asked that question.) Those who pay "all" or "nothing" are assumed to have employee shares of 100 percent or zero, respectively. Probability tables based on the MEPS-IC and conditioned on firm size, industry, and full- or part-time employment status are used to impute the employer and employee shares of the total premium for those who pay "some." More general tables from the MEPS are used to impute "shadow" employer and employee premium shares for workers who are not policyholders in the base case but who might choose to take up coverage under various policy scenarios.

## Nongroup Premiums

Nongroup premiums are created using a structure similar to that used for ESI premiums. The key difference is that premiums are not averaged within a firm—the individual premium is based more on an individual's expected health costs. The age–sex and health factors are identical to those described for ESI, although in this case the factors have more direct implications for the cost of the premium because the factors are not averaged across a group of coworkers. For example, a person who is in fair health (the factor is 1.9) is assigned a premium that is nearly double the premium that would be charged someone of the same age and sex who is in excellent health. The health factors in general are consistent with observed nongroup underwriting practices; people with preexisting health conditions often pay more for the same coverage, and in some states it is legal to deny nongroup coverage to a person with a preexisting condition.[5] The model does not use an experience factor because experience rating is relatively rare in the nongroup market.

The loading factor is a significant ingredient in creating nongroup premiums. It constitutes a large proportion—about 29 percent, on average—of the total premium. The large factor reflects various aspects of the nongroup market, including the fact that it enjoys far fewer economies of scale than does the ESI market.

### *Relative Plan Value and Base Premium*

Nongroup policies usually have lower relative plan values than do employer-sponsored policies. Data from several surveys suggest a mean premium of $2,900 in 2004 for a single nongroup policy.[6] That premium is slightly higher than the average premium that would be charged the general population because current nongroup policyholders are older, on average, than is the nonelderly population at large and older than ESI policyholders.

Given that age difference and the higher loading costs for nongroup policies (about 29 percent of premiums), observed premiums would be higher than those for ESI, all else being equal. However, ESI premiums averaged roughly $3,700 in 2004, implying that once differences in the characteristics of nongroup versus ESI policyholders are considered and different loading costs are considered, a typical nongroup policy has roughly 60 percent of the relative plan value of an average ESI policy. That finding is supported by a recent survey of nongroup and ESI premiums and relative plan values in California.[7]

### *Effects of State Regulation*

The extensive regulation of underwriting practices in the nongroup market, as in the small-group ESI market, can dramatically affect premiums. For example, many states impose rating bands to allow some, but not unlimited, variation in premiums to correspond to subscribers' age or health status: If the rating band for health status is 2:1, nongroup premiums for otherwise identical individuals who differ only in health status cannot vary by more than a factor of 2. In the model, the health factor is truncated (in a way that preserves the average health factor) so that the factor for those in the poorest health is exactly twice that for those in the best health. Thus, premiums are compressed (with the healthiest people paying more and the sickest paying less) relative to premiums in states without rating regulations.

In states that require pure community rating for nongroup premiums, the same premium is charged for every individual in the model. As in the cases of more limited rating regulations, premiums are set such that if all rating restrictions were removed, the aggregate of premiums collected would be the same as if the restrictions were in place (if the same population remained insured).

Family nongroup premiums are constructed by adding the individual premiums of all potential family members and computing a 5 percent discount for each additional member beyond the policyholder to reflect administrative savings on such costs as marketing and brokers' fees.

The modeled distributions of single premiums for ESI and nongroup coverage show the effect of pooling in firms—nongroup premiums vary more than ESI premiums do. Although the mean premium for nongroup coverage is projected to be lower than that for ESI in 2008 because of lower relative plan value (roughly $3,700 versus $5,200), the highest nongroup premiums exceed the highest ESI premiums.

## Adjustments to Premiums for Tax Benefits

People who purchase insurance through an employer receive a tax benefit, as do self-employed workers who purchase their own plans. Payments by employers for health insurance are excluded from workers' taxable income for income and payroll taxes, and employers may treat their contributions to premiums as a tax-deductible business expense. In most cases, the share of ESI premiums paid by workers also is excluded from taxable income. Self-employed people are allowed to deduct payments they make for health insurance.

CBO's model assumes that firms and individuals behave as if they consider that tax advantage in making their insurance decisions. Thus, a premium adjusted for tax savings, or a *net premium,* is calculated alongside the premium as described above to represent the amount of forgone spending on goods other than health insurance. The net premium is calculated using marginal tax rates imputed to each SIPP respondent through TAXSIM, a tax simulation computer model developed and maintained by the National Bureau of Economic Research.[8]

Consider an individual with a 25 percent total marginal tax rate (including federal, state, and payroll taxes) who holds a single ESI policy with a total premium of $4,000 and an employee contribution of $1,000. The employer contribution of $3,000 is excluded from reportable income, saving the employee $750 (25 percent of $3,000). Most employees (about 85 percent) also pay their share of premiums with before-tax income. In this example, the employee would save an additional $250 (25 percent of $1,000). In simulating the employee's purchasing behavior, the CBO model uses the net premium of $3,000 (the net employer contribution is $2,250 and the net employee contribution is $750). The model also adjusts net nongroup premiums downward for self-employed purchasers because they are entitled to an income tax deduction. On average, for ESI, net premiums are roughly 27 percent lower than are nominal premiums for single ESI policyholders. For nongroup policyholders, net premiums are 10 percent below nominal premiums, on average.

## End Notes

[1] Although individuals in the SIPP report their health status, they do not report health expenditures. Thus, the MEPS expenditure data are imputed to the SIPP survey respondents

by "hot decking," the random assignment to SIPP respondents of health expenditures from similar groups of individuals observed in the MEPS, based on age, sex, past health care utilization, and insurance status.

[2] Actuarial Research Corporation, *Study of the Administrative Costs and Actuarial Values of Small Health Plans* (prepared for the Small Business Administration Office of Advocacy, January 2003).

[3] See General Accounting Office, *Health Insurance Regulation: Varying State Requirements Affect Cost of Insurance,* GAO/HEHS-96-161 (August 1996), www.gao.gov/archive/1996/he96161.pdf. Regulations obtained from this source have been updated with information from several unpublished sources.

[4] Data on differences by firm size are taken from Actuarial Research Corporation, *Study of the Administrative Costs and Actuarial Values of Small Health Plans.* Differences in relative plan value by income and health status are based, in part, on Mark Pauly, "The Demand for Health Insurance in the Group Setting: Can You Always Get What You Want?" *Journal of Risk & Insurance,* vol. 74, no. 1 (2007), pp. 115–140.

[5] See Congressional Budget Office, *The Price Sensitivity of Demand for Nongroup Health Insurance (August 2005); and Mark Merlis, Fundamentals of Underwriting in the Nongroup Health Insurance Market: Access to Coverage and Options for Reform,* National Health Policy Forum Background Paper (Washington, D.C.: George Washington University, April 2005), www.nhpf.org/pdfs_bp/ BP_Underwriting_04-13-05.pdf.

[6] Some premium information comes from the AHIP Center for Policy and Research, *Individual Health Insurance: A Comprehensive Survey of Affordability, Access, and Benefits* (Washington, D.C.: America's Health Insurance Plans, August 2005), www.ahipresearch.org/bytopic.html. Additional estimates are from the National Health Interview Survey (Bradley Herring, Emory University, September 2005, personal communication); from unpublished estimates from the Medical Expenditure Panel Survey and eHealth Insurance; and from Sherry Glied and Sarah Little, "The Price of Health Insurance: Modeling Premiums in Models of Insurance Expansions" (paper presented at an Academy Health conference, "Determinants of Premiums in the Individual Market," Washington, D.C., November 12, 2003).

[7] Jon Gabel and others, "Trends in the Golden State: Small-Group Premiums Rise Sharply While Actuarial Values for Individual Coverage Plummet," *Health Affairs,* Web exclusive, vol. 26, no. 4 (2007), w488–w499.

[8] TAXSIM is available online from the National Bureau of Economic Research: www.nber.org/~taxsim. See also Daniel Feenberg and Elisabeth Coutts, "An Introduction to the TAXSIM Model," Journal of Policy Analysis and Management, vol. 12, no. 1 (1993), pp. 189–194, www.nber.org/~taxsim/feenberg-coutts.pdf.

In: A Health Insurance Model for Analyzing... ISBN: 978-1-60741-052-2
Editor: Alan S. Burley 

*Chapter 7*

# CALIBRATION

***Congressional Budget Office***

CBO's model is calibrated to match demographic, financial, and health insurance characteristics of the U.S. population for 2008 through 2017. The model matches the Census Bureau's projections (by age, sex, and race) of the noninstitutionalized U.S. population by adjusting the sample weight of each SIPP observation. Institutionalized individuals (nursing home residents and prisoners, for example) are excluded because they are not included in the SIPP and unlikely in any case to be included in efforts to expand health insurance coverage. (Table 1 displays the population characteristics that were used to calibrate CBO's model.)

The sample weights are further adjusted to match estimates of the uninsured population and estimates of the type of coverage held by those who are insured. CBO's estimate of the number of uninsured people originates with a point-in-time, SIPP-based estimate in 2002. Some demographic groups, among them Hispanics, have lower rates of health insurance participation than the general population does. The number of people in those groups is expected to increase faster than the general population. Thus, the adjustments to the SIPP weights to match the changing demographics of the U.S. population result in an increase in the number of uninsured individuals (as a percentage of the U.S. population) over the period between 2008 and 2017.

CBO also adjusted the model to correct survey inaccuracies in estimating the number of people with and without health insurance coverage. According to recent research, many survey respondents who are covered by Medicaid mistakenly report being uninsured or being covered by some other type of health insurance.[1] As a result, survey-based estimates of the number of Medicaid enrollees are significantly lower than the number estimated from Medicaid administrative data. Using the results of that research, CBO adjusted upward the number of people in its model who are on Medicaid and adjusted downward the number who are uninsured and the number who report other types of coverage. Thus, the number of Medicaid enrollees in the model is higher than typically reported in survey data, and the number of uninsured people is lower.[2] In its projections of SCHIP enrollment through 2017, CBO's model assumes that additional SCHIP funding will be provided to maintain current programs, adjusted for changes in population and the uninsured. (Under baseline funding levels, by contrast, CBO projects that SCHIP enrollment will decline with available funding.)

**Table 1. Population Characteristics Used to Calibrate CBO's Health Insurance Simulation Model, Various Years**

| | Population (Millions)[a] | | | Percentage of Population | | |
|---|---|---|---|---|---|---|
| | **2002** | **2008** | **2017** | **2002** | **2008** | **2017** |
| Sex | | | | | | |
| Female | 144.5 | 152.6 | 164.5 | 51 | 51 | 51 |
| Male | 138.9 | 146.7 | 158.2 | 49 | 49 | 49 |
| Age | | | | | | |
| 0 to 18 | 77.2 | 79.5 | 83.9 | 27 | 27 | 26 |
| 19 to 24 | 23.5 | 24.8 | 24.8 | 8 | 8 | 8 |
| 25 to 44 | 82.6 | 81.2 | 84.0 | 29 | 27 | 26 |
| 45 to 64 | 65.9 | 76.6 | 82.3 | 23 | 26 | 26 |
| 65 and older | 34.1 | 37.1 | 47.7 | 12 | 12 | 15 |
| Race or Ethnicity | | | | | | |
| White, non-Hispanic | 194.7 | 197.1 | 200.8 | 69 | 66 | 62 |
| Nonwhite, non-Hispanic | 51.2 | 56.7 | 65.5 | 18 | 19 | 20 |
| Hispanic | 37.5 | 45.4 | 56.4 | 13 | 15 | 17 |
| Uninsured Under Age 65[b] | 39.4 | 44.2 | 49.7 | 16 | 17 | 18 |
| **Total Population** | **283.4** | **299.2** | **322.7** | **100** | **100** | **100** |

Sources: Congressional Budget Office; Bureau of the Census.

a. The population considered is the total U.S. noninstitutionalized population.

b. Estimates are for nonelderly people who do not have health insurance at a given point in the year, as a percentage of the total U.S. nonelderly population.

The research literature suggests that real (inflation adjusted) growth in average health insurance premiums results in a larger number of people without health insurance, so the model's weights were further modified to reflect the influence of premium growth, from 2008 to 2017, on the number of uninsured people.[3] In the absence of any consideration of real growth in average premiums, CBO's model projects that the uninsured nonelderly population would increase from 15.8 percent of nonelderly U.S. residents in 2002 to 16.7 percent in 2017. Including premium growth in that calculation leads to a projection of 18.1 percent in 2017.

The number of people with private health insurance coverage is the total population less the sum of the projected number of people without health insurance and the projected number of people with public health coverage. Adjustments to all types of private insurance were made proportionally. For ESI, CBO relied on data from the 2003 MEPS-IC, which showed about 89 million people holding ESI policies in 2003. CBO used that starting point and projected ESI enrollment to grow at a rate that matches that for total private health insurance. Thus, CBO estimated that 90 million people would hold ESI policies in 2008 and 93 million would be policyholders in 2017. Those projections are incorporated into the adjusted weights.

The final calibrations involve adjustments to financial data, including wage income, total income, health expenditures, and health insurance premiums. Income variables were adjusted to match CBO's baseline for national income. Health expenditures were imputed from MEPS based on the SIPP data for age, sex, health status, medical utilization, health insurance coverage, and, if covered by ESI, employer size. To account for the MEPS undercounts of people with extremely high medical costs, the imputed expenditures were adjusted to match the distribution observed in the Society of Actuaries' Large Claims Data Set. Expenditures were then adjusted to match projections reported in the NHEAs for each year from 2008 to 2017. Private health insurance premiums (created as described above) were set such that total private premiums matched appropriate totals derived from the NHEAs. The trends in annual average premium growth were derived from NHEA data.

The base case distribution of coverage status among the nonelderly population (shown in Table 2) is consistent with other major surveys. Roughly 62 percent of the nonelderly population will be covered by employer-sponsored insurance in 2008 and about 17 percent of the nonelderly population will be uninsured. (The totals in Table 2 add to more than 100 percent because some respondents in the samples reported having more than one type of coverage simultaneously.)

**Table 2. Baseline Health Insurance Coverage of the Nonelderly Population, 2008**

| | Nonelderly Population | |
|---|---|---|
| | **Millions** | **Percent[a]** |
| Insured | | |
| ESI, single | 37.6 | 14.4 |
| ESI, family[b] | 124.8 | 47.6 |
| Nongroup, single | 4.2 | 1.6 |
| Nongroup, family[b] | 6.0 | 2.3 |
| Medicare | 5.8 | 2.2 |
| Medicaid and SCHIP | 42.1 | 16.1 |
| TRICARE[c] | 11.5 | 4.4 |
| Uninsured | 44.2 | 16.9 |

Source: Congressional Budget Office's health insurance simulation model based on data from the Bureau of the Census's Survey of Income and Program Participation.

Notes: ESI = employer-sponsored insurance; SCHIP = State Children's Health Insurance Program. Figures are for coverage status of the nonelderly population in a typical month in 2008.

a. The sum of the percentages of the nonelderly population exceeds 100 because of multiple coverage.

b. Includes dependent coverage.

c. TRICARE is the Department of Defense's health care system.

## End Notes

[1] Michael Davern, Jacob Alex Klerman, and Jeanette Ziegenfuss, *Medicaid Under-Reporting in the Current Population Survey and One Approach for a Partial Correction* (Minneapolis, Minnesota: University of Minnesota State Health Access Data Assistance Center, October 15, 2007), http:// cps.ipums.org/cps/medadjust.pdf.

[2] The model's estimated enrollment in major public health-financing programs—Medicare, Medicaid, and SCHIP—is not the same as that published annually in CBO's March baseline. The annual baseline reports all enrollees, whereas CBO's microsimulation model does not include enrollees who are institutionalized, many of whom are covered by Medicare, Medicaid, or both. In addition, the CBO enrollment baseline reports the number of people who are enrolled for one or more months during a given fiscal year; the model reports average monthly enrollment.

[3] See Michael Chernew, David M. Cutler, and Patricia Seliger Keenan, "Increasing Health Insurance Costs and the Decline in Insurance Coverage," *Health Services Research,* vol. 40, no. 4 (2005), pp. 1021–1039, www.blackwell-synergy.com/doi/pdf/10.1111/j.1475-6773.2005.00409 .x?cookieSet=1.

In: A Health Insurance Model for Analyzing... ISBN: 978-1-60741-052-2
Editor: Alan S. Burley 

*Chapter 8*

# BEHAVIORAL RESPONSES

***Congressional Budget Office***

CBO uses its health insurance model to simulate the results of a variety of legislative proposals that would affect the number of U.S. residents who do not have health insurance. The legislative options include subsidies or tax incentives for the purchase of private insurance, health savings accounts, reinsurance, regulatory changes that affect underwriting practices, changes to Medicaid or SCHIP eligibility rules, and employer mandates for offering coverage or individual mandates for purchasing coverage. The model considers the effect that changes to Medicaid or SCHIP eligibility rules would have on employer offers and private insurance take-up rates, but it does not simulate the effects of proposals that would primarily expand Medicaid or SCHIP eligibility. CBO is exploring ways to add the capacity to model such proposals.

In: A Health Insurance Model for Analyzing... ISBN: 978-1-60741-052-2
Editor: Alan S. Burley 

*Chapter 9*

# CHANGES IN RELATIVE PLAN VALUE

## *Congressional Budget Office*

In CBO's model, changes in the unit price of health insurance (the cost per dollar of coverage) affect the desired relative plan value. Subsidies that are based on a percentage of the premium affect that unit price, as do many changes in the tax treatment of health insurance. For example, someone with a 25 percent marginal tax rate could purchase $1 of fully deductible health insurance coverage with 75 cents of after-tax expenditure. If that tax deduction was removed, each dollar of premium purchased would be 25 cents more expensive, and the subscriber would be expected to purchase less coverage.

Fixed-dollar subsidies, by contrast, would have little effect on relative plan value because they do not change the unit price of the insurance. (Under a fixed-dollar subsidy, an additional dollar of health insurance has the same price it did before.) Fixed-dollar subsidies could affect relative plan value, however, if they exceeded the unsubsidized premium. By not purchasing more extensive coverage (for example, in a plan with a lower deductible), subscribers effectively leave subsidy dollars "on the table." Typical proposals of this type include a required actuarial value to qualify for the subsidy.

To estimate the extent to which the relative plan value would change as a result of a change in the unit price of insurance, the model uses an elasticity of relative plan value. That elasticity is assumed to be –0.35, on average (similar to the estimate by Jonathan Gruber and Michael Lettau).[1] In the case of a 10 percent premium increase, the elasticity produces a 3.5 percent reduction in relative plan value for people who continue to hold ESI policies. Small firms and low-income purchasers of health insurance are assumed to be more responsive to unit price changes in health insurance and are assigned relatively larger elasticities, which is consistent with data in the literature.

## End Note

1 Jonathan Gruber and Michael Lettau, "How Elastic Is the Firm's Demand for Health Insurance?" *Journal of Public Economics,* vol. 88, nos. 7–8 (2004), pp. 1273–1293.

In: A Health Insurance Model for Analyzing… ISBN: 978-1-60741-052-2
Editor: Alan S. Burley 

*Chapter 10*

# EMPLOYER BEHAVIOR

## *Congressional Budget Office*

The driving principle of CBO's modeling of employer behavior is that businesses compete for workers by offering wage and benefit packages that will attract and help retain employees. Employers offer health insurance (and other benefits) if they believe their employees want such coverage enough, in effect, to trade cash wages for it. The fact that some fringe benefits either are not taxable compensation or confer other tax advantages makes them an attractive way to compensate workers, especially high-wage workers, whose higher marginal tax rates allow the largest effective subsidies for fringe benefits. The synthetic firms in CBO's model may cease (or begin) offering ESI to their employees if conditions change such that offering insurance becomes less (or more) advantageous as a result of a policy or market change.

### Employer Decisions to Offer Insurance

Changes in the after-tax cost of insurance can influence an employer's decision to offer a health plan. For example, a change in that cost that is attributable to a new tax policy, revised state regulations, or alterations in direct government subsidies can induce an employer to reevaluate its ESI policy.

The effects of premium changes are modeled by multiplying the average change for a firm's employees by an elasticity of offer with respect to the premium to arrive at the likelihood that the firm will start or stop offering the coverage. The elasticity varies with the size of the firm (see Table 3) and is based on several estimates derived from the literature (see Appendix A).[1] The resulting value is in the form of a probability of offer, which is then assigned to the worker.

Consider, for example, a hypothetical small business. The company has fewer than 25 employees, and currently it does not offer ESI. The effect of a policy proposal to subsidize the purchase of ESI by 25 percent would be a price change, –0.25, multiplied by –1.14 (the take-up elasticity of offer for very small firms). The likelihood that the employer in this case would begin to offer ESI is 28.5 percent.

The employer's decision to start or stop offering coverage also is affected by changes in the relative attractiveness of alternatives to ESI, such as nongroup or Medicaid coverage. CBO generally assumes that a firm is less likely to offer coverage if its employees' outside insurance options become more attractive relative to ESI. The magnitude of those effects is assumed to be roughly one-quarter to one-half as large as the direct effect of ESI premiums. Thus, a 10 percent reduction in nongroup premiums available to a firm's employees would increase the likelihood of that firm's dropping coverage to the same extent that a 2.5 percent to 5 percent increase in the firm's ESI premiums would cause it to drop coverage.

This effect is similar to a traditional cross-price elasticity: the effect on the quantity purchased of product A as a function of changes in the price of substitute product B. Because ESI and nongroup coverage are not perfect substitutes, this effect is smaller than is the effect of an ESI price change on the ESI offer decision. The analogy also is imperfect: The firm is not in fact purchasing nongroup coverage for its employees—it is merely returning what it had previously paid as its contributions to ESI coverage in the form of wages or other fringe benefits while leaving to its employees the decision of whether and how to obtain health insurance.

Firms whose employees have high marginal tax rates are assumed to be less sensitive to changes in nongroup premiums or to eligibility for Medicaid or SCHIP, as are firms whose ESI premiums would be substantially lower than the nongroup premiums their employees would pay, even after a reduction in those premiums. That is, holding benefits constant, the model also considers not just the change in the average ESI or non-group premiums for employees, but which option is less expensive (and by how much) before and after the change in policy.

**Table 3. Offer Elasticities and Offer Rates by Firm Size, 2008, in CBO's Model**

| | | Offered and Eligible for ESI | | | Offered ESI with Premium Increase[a] | |
|---|---|---|---|---|---|---|
| **Firm Size** | **Employees (Millions)** | **Number (Millions)** | **Percent** | **Elasticity of Offer[b]** | **Number (Millions)** | **Percent** |
| Under 25 | 27.7 | 12.1 | 43.9 | -1.14 | 10.8 | 38.9 |
| 25 to 99 | 16.1 | 11.4 | 70.9 | -0.38 | 11.0 | 68.2 |
| 100 to 999[c] | 25.3 | 19.5 | 77.2 | -0.15 | 19.2 | 76.1 |
| 1,000-Plus[c] | 59.2 | 50.6 | 85.4 | 0 | 50.6 | 85.4 |
| **All** | **128.2** | **93.6** | **73.0** | **-0.22** | **91.6** | **71.5** |

Source: Congressional Budget Office's health insurance simulation model.
Note: ESI = employer-sponsored insurance.

a. Employees' premiums would increase by 10 percent.

b. See Appendix A for a definition of elasticity of offer.

c. Firms of this size are not identified in the Bureau of the Census's Survey of Income and Program Participation. Rather, they are subgroups created by random assignment from within the 100-plus category.

Although most employers find that ESI is more economical because of its lower administrative costs, there are cases in which nongroup coverage could be less expensive. Consider a case in which healthy employees of a small firm are subject to rate compression regulations in the ESI market. If they are eligible for subsidies and subject to less rate compression in the nongroup market, it might be to their benefit for their employer to stop offering ESI, adjust their wages accordingly, and leave them free to purchase nongroup coverage on their own.

Finally, the model assumes nonlinear responses to changes in premiums. Employers whose employees would receive a 50 percent subsidy for nongroup premiums are modeled as being more than five times as responsive as employers whose employees have a 10 percent reduction in nongroup premiums.

## Changes in Employer Contributions

The model uses three basic assumptions to simulate changes in employers' contributions to health insurance premiums in response to a proposal to expand health insurance. First, employers generally act to maximize the subsidies they and their workers receive from the government (consistent with the overall assumption of this component that employers seek to maximize employee utility). Second, although employers keep the cost of employee compensation fixed, they may change the proportion of compensation allocated for health care benefits and the portion paid in cash wages and other fringe benefits. Finally, employers reduce their contributions to premiums somewhat if outside insurance options become more attractive to their workforce, although employers do not make compensation adjustments with perfect accuracy.

The last assumption is founded on empirical work published by researchers who report that employers tend to raise employee contributions in response to increased Medicaid eligibility among their employees.[2] By simultaneously raising the employee contribution and lowering the employer contribution toward ESI premiums, the employer makes it more attractive for low-income workers to enroll in a public program—those workers are not forgoing as much of an employer contribution when they decline the employer's plan.

Some employers might react the opposite way, however: Increasingly attractive outside insurance options might lead them to raise their premium contributions—and reduce the amount their employees contribute—as a way to induce healthy workers to stay in the firm's risk pool.[3] That is more of a possibility in the case of fixed-dollar nongroup subsidies that would more likely attract healthier workers who would pay lower after-subsidy premiums. CBO's model assumes the former effect is dominant, but offset somewhat by the latter, and thus a relatively small effect is used.

In the case of a direct premium subsidy for ESI, the CBO model assumes that employers adjust the employees' contributions in proportion to the premium subsidy that goes to the company's average worker. If the subsidy goes directly to the worker (for example, if a check is mailed to the employee each month), the assumption is that the employer would raise the employee's contribution. In most cases, the increase would equal about half the amount of the subsidy. Most employers require some contribution for ESI coverage, even if that will diminish the tax subsidy available to workers (one theory is that some employers require a substantial employee contribution such that employees who have no interest in the employer's plan can save money by not contributing). If the employee contribution is subsidized, many businesses will raise the amount employees pay to ensure that workers continue to contribute some amount. Likewise, in the case of a subsidy going directly to the employer, the model assumes employers will raise their contributions in response, but not by the full amount of the subsidy.

## End Notes

[1] Gruber and Lettau, "How Elastic Is the Firm's Demand for Health Insurance?"; Jack Hadley and James D. Reschovsky, "Small Firms' Demand for Health Insurance: The Decision to Offer Insurance," *Inquiry,* vol. 39, no. 2 (2002), pp. 118–137; and Len Nichols and Linda J. Blumberg, "Estimating Employer Elasticity of Demand for Health Insurance" (paper presented at Academy Health Annual Research Meeting, Washington, D.C., 1999).

[2] See Thomas C. Buchmueller and others, "The Effect of SCHIP Expansions on Health Insurance Decisions by Employers," *Inquiry,* vol. 42, no. 3 (2005), pp. 218–231; and Jonathan Gruber and Robin McKnight, "Why Did Employee Health Insurance Contributions Rise?" *Journal of Health Economics,* vol. 22, no. 6 (2003), pp. 1085–1104.

[3] See Sherry Glied and Joshua Graff Zivin, *Modeling Employer Decisions to Offer Health Insurance,* Robert Wood Johnson Foundation Working Paper (Princeton, N.J.: Robert Wood Johnson Foundation, revised August 2004), www.rwjf.org/pr/synthesis/reports_ and_briefs/pdf/no7 _researchabstract.pdf.

In: A Health Insurance Model for Analyzing... ISBN: 978-1-60741-052-2
Editor: Alan S. Burley 

*Chapter 11*

# INDIVIDUAL COVERAGE RESPONSES

***Congressional Budget Office***

The CBO model simulates the responses of individual workers to changes in the cost of premiums, to changes in their employers' offers of employer-sponsored insurance, and to changes in eligibility for Medicaid or SCHIP. Matching what is observed in practice, the model has most workers with families taking up family coverage rather than single coverage. However, the model does allow for workers with families to take up single coverage with some probability in cases where there is a financial incentive to do so. Specifically, the probabilities of take-up of single and family coverage are computed independently, and the single-coverage take-up is set equal to the probability of single take-up minus the probability of family take-up. If the computation results in a 30 percent probability of family coverage and a 40 percent probability of single coverage for a single parent, for example, the parent's single-coverage likelihood is set at 10 percent (40 percent minus 30 percent). Thus, that parent has a 60 percent chance and the children have a 70 percent chance of being uninsured. The transitions between coverage states are discussed below.

## Uninsured People Who Take Up Nongroup Coverage

Because they would provide direct subsidies or regulatory changes, many policy scenarios would result in lower nongroup premiums. Thus, one crucial pathway to consider is the one that takes uninsured people to nongroup coverage. The key parameter is the nongroup premium elasticity, which can be expressed as the percentage of individuals who would take up nongroup coverage for a given percentage reduction in the nongroup premium. Several studies have attempted to estimate that elasticity by observing how people facing lower nongroup insurance premiums behave differently from those facing higher premiums. (Some research groups have examined geographic differences in premiums as their source of observed premium variation, and in a separate study, CBO has made use of differences in state regulations).[1] The estimates suggest that, in exchange for a 25 percent reduction in the nongroup premium, 2 percent to 6 percent of the uninsured population would take up coverage; for a 50 percent price reduction, the range increases to 4 percent to 20 percent.[2]

The literature may not be a useful guide for subsidies that are much above 50 percent; observed premium variation above that level is rare. Thus, CBO chose to estimate the enrollment response to a 100 percent subsidy based on observed participation rates in free public programs and to fit a response function that satisfies the elasticity results both for smaller subsidies and for the estimated response to a 100 percent subsidy. CBO's model uses a two-part response function, shown in Expressions (1) and (2).

When the reduction in the premium is 50 percent or less, the probability of take-up can be expressed as follows:

$$0.3 \times \%\Delta P \times IE \qquad (1)$$

When the premium is reduced by more than 50 percent, the probability of take-up is

$$[0.15 + (\%\Delta P - 0.5)^2 \times 2.6] \times IE \qquad (2)$$

In Expressions (1) and (2), $\%\Delta P$ is the percentage reduction in the premium and $IE$ is the income effect, which is defined as

$$(1 - P_{net}/I)^{1.5} \qquad (3)$$

where $P_{net}$ is the postsubsidy premium payment and $I$ is income.

The income effect reflects the fact that high-income workers have higher take-up rates, at any given subsidy amount, than low-income workers do. As subsidies approach 100 percent, the take-up rates of high- and low-income workers converge.[3] The effect of that function is to reduce take-up rates, for example, by 15 percent if new premium payments equal 10 percent of annual income, by 35 percent if premiums equal 25 percent of income, and by 65 percent if premiums equal half of income. The same income effect is used in all scenarios that involve a net increase in premium payments.

Figure 2 illustrates the overall take-up rate for nongroup coverage among nonelderly workers without access to ESI or to public coverage, as a function of the proportion of the premium covered by the subsidy. Under current law, which is assumed to be zero-subsidy, about 20 percent of that population has nongroup coverage.

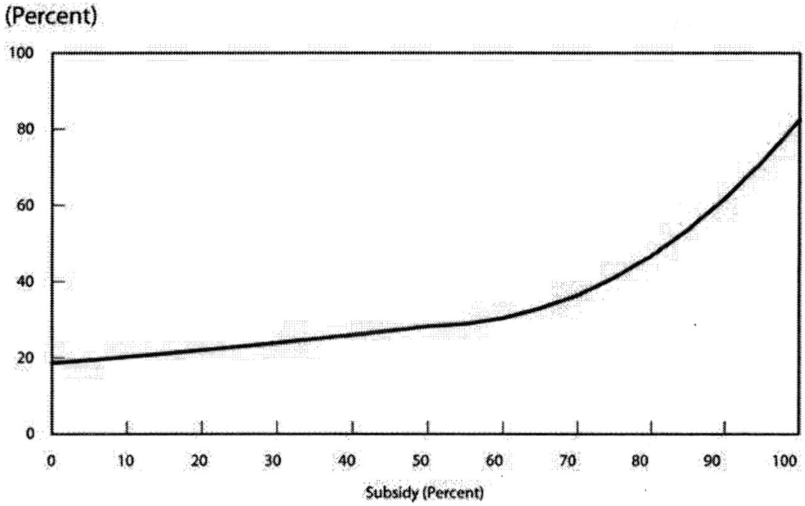


Source: Congressional Budget Office's health insurance simulation model.

Note: Roughly 32 million nonelderly U.S. residents lack access to an offer of employer-sponsored insurance and are ineligible for Medicaid or the State Children's Health Insurance Program. The curve displays the estimated probability of take-up of nongroup coverage in that population as a function of a subsidy set at a percentage of the insurance premium.

Figure 2. Probability of Take-Up of Nongroup Insurance

CBO's model further adjusts the take-up response to account for variations in the responses to subsidies among different subgroups of uninsured people.[4] In general, the model assumes that uninsured individuals who have other options they have not taken up (such as Medicaid or ESI) also have a lower take-up probability for non-group subsidies. Similarly, uninsured parents whose children have public coverage are assumed to be slightly less likely to take up family nongroup or ESI coverage, and the likelihood is reduced in proportion to the percentage of children on public coverage.

## Uninsured People Who Take Up ESI

Take-up of employer-sponsored insurance among the uninsured is modeled with the same general principles used for nongroup coverage, although it is varied according to whether the worker is responding only to a change in the required employee contribution or to a new offer of ESI.

The probability of an uninsured person—with an existing ESI offer—taking up ESI with a new subsidy is described by Expression (4):[5]

$$(0.4 \times \%\Delta P + 0.2 \times \%\Delta P^2) \times IE \qquad (4)$$

where $P$ refers only to the employee's contribution to the ESI premium. Workers are more responsive to changes in the employee share of the premium—the part that they actually pay—than they are to changes in the total premium.

There is a more extensive literature on Expression (4) than there is for nongroup take-up, although there is considerable variation in the results reported. For example, a 25 percent reduction in an employee premium corresponds to a new take-up rate reported at just over 1 percent (by Jonathan Gruber and Ebonya Washington), 8 percent (Linda Blumberg and others; Anne Royalty and John Hagens), 15 percent (Michael Chernew and others), or nearly 20 percent (in a study of the near-elderly by Thomas Buchmueller and Sabina Ohri).[6] (Those take-up rates refer to the minority of employees who had not already taken up coverage. In general, 80 percent of employees who are offered ESI take up coverage.)

The estimates cited from the literature are based on different approaches to studying the behavioral response to changes in the employee contribution. In particular, Royalty and Hagens used hypothetical questions posed to employees about their willingness to pay. The estimate developed by Gruber and Washington, which was based on changes in the tax excludability of employee contributions, may be smaller than the others because tax-based changes in premium contributions may be less transparent to employees or discounted because the savings are realized only when taxes are filed. (CBO's model can be modified to consider the mechanism by which a subsidy is offered.)

Unlike the case of nongroup premiums, one can readily observe cases in which employees would receive a 100 percent subsidy for ESI (that is, the employee contribution to the premium would be zero). It is well known that even in such cases, when employees would not be subject to any additional premium payments if they took up the employer's plan, a significant percentage of employees still do not take up coverage and some are uninsured. For example, the employees might have a strong preference against coverage or they could be covered as dependents on other policies. Based on those cases and the above-cited studies, Expression (4) assumes that at least 40 percent of those who decline ESI and are uninsured in the base case would remain uninsured (implying a maximum take-up of 60 percent) even if their contributions to the premiums were eliminated completely.

As noted above, the proportion of the potential ESI market that is insured through ESI is larger than the potential nongroup market that is insured through nongroup coverage—at any subsidy (see Figure 3). The lower price sensitivity of ESI take-up compared with nongroup take-up primarily reflects the greater value of ESI (attributable to tax subsidies, lower administrative loading, lower search costs, premiums that are less sensitive to individual health status, and the direct payment of a portion of the premium by employers through wage reductions).

Take-up among uninsured workers who receive new offers of ESI as a result of a change in policy also is modeled with Expression (4), but with one important differ- ence. Absent any price incentive (that is, if the employee's premium contribution were equal to the nongroup premium available before the new offer), the offer of ESI by itself is assumed to induce a 50 percent likelihood of take-up. That assumption is consistent with the discussion above and follows from empirical research that estimates coverage rates as a function of the percentage of the premium contributed by employers. Take-up is further adjusted to account for the employee's contribution relative to the nongroup premium available before the ESI offer is made.

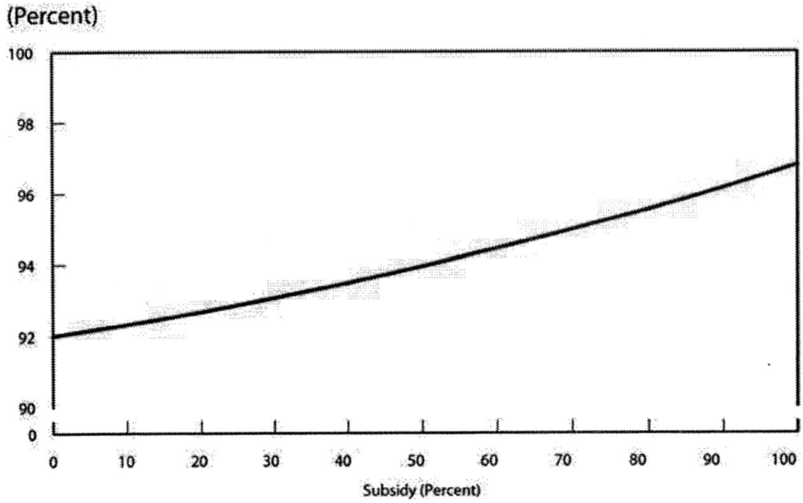


Source: Congressional Budget Office's health insurance simulation model.

Note: Roughly 155 million nonelderly U.S. residents have access to an offer of employer-sponsored insurance and are ineligible for Medicaid or the State Children's Health Insurance Program. The curve displays the estimated probability of take-up of coverage in that population as a function of a subsidy set at a percentage of the employee portion of the insurance premium.

Figure 3. Probability of Take-Up of Employer-Sponsored Insurance

## ESI-Insured People Who Become Uninsured

There are two pathways by which people with ESI may become uninsured. In the first case, workers lose access to ESI when employers discontinue coverage. In the long run, workers who lost an ESI offer would see an increase in their cash wages that would equal, on average, their employers' cost of providing health insurance. However, because demand for health insurance is relatively unresponsive to small changes in income, CBO did not incorporate that potential wage increase into its modeling of take-up. All changes in income are reflected in calculations of the consequences for federal tax revenues.

Upon losing an ESI offer, workers generally consider several fallback options: First, there is a high probability that a spouse would reconsider and accept a preexisting family ESI offer that had previously been declined.

Alternatively, the worker might elect nongroup coverage. The latter option is less likely if the nongroup premium is high or if the individual is in good health (and thus believes purchasing health insurance is not necessary). The worker also could choose to enroll in Medicaid if eligible. The probability of choosing that option declines if the worker is in good health. If none of the options is taken, the worker becomes uninsured.

The second pathway to becoming uninsured occurs in response to an increase in the employee's premium contribution, with no change in the employer's offer status. In the case of a change in policy, an increase in the employee contribution might be attributable to one or more of several factors, including a reduction in the ESI tax benefit, a new tax on premiums, or an increase in the share of the total premium that employees must pay. Employees are assumed to drop coverage as a function of the premium increase such that, for example, a 20 percent increase in the contribution—from $1,000 to $1,200 (where the total premium is $4,000)—results in roughly 1 percent of those enrolled dropping ESI coverage. That approximates the finding in the literature of roughly a –0.05 elasticity.

## People Who Switch Between ESI and Nongroup Coverage

It is reasonable to assume that some workers would switch coverage based entirely on the relative prices of ESI and nongroup coverage. For example, if a single male pays an employee contribution of $2,000, but a subsidy lowers the nongroup premium for equivalent coverage from $2,500 to $1,500, he is assumed to treat the new nongroup offer as a 25 percent subsidy ($2,000 less $1,500 divided by $2,000) and to take up nongroup coverage in a way that matches that of otherwise uninsured individuals presented with a 25 percent subsidy for nongroup coverage. The employee portion of the premium is used (rather than the total premium) because it is assumed that if he dropped ESI coverage, he would retain only that portion as cash. It is assumed that any future wage increases would not reflect the forgone contribution the employer would make to the premium.

Because of the loss of the employer contribution to premiums, greater loading in non-group coverage, and higher search costs, that sort of switching is not expected to be very common. According to the data underlying the base case, only about 1 percent of nonelderly people who are offered ESI are instead covered by nongroup insurance. Nevertheless, large subsidies for nongroup coverage could induce some people—especially those in relatively good health who might pay higher ESI premiums because they were pooled with less healthy coworkers—to leave ESI for nongroup coverage.

## Private-Coverage Take-Up among Those Who Are Eligible for or Enrolled in Medicaid or SCHIP

Finally, CBO's model examines how some people with Medicaid or SCHIP coverage might take up ESI or nongroup coverage if the cost fell or if they became ineligible to participate in either of those programs.

If in the former case there was a new incentive or subsidy for private coverage, even though the individual might have to pay a premium or copayment, it is assumed that avoiding the possible stigma associated with participation in a means-tested, public program and possibly improving access to health care would prompt some people to switch from Medicaid or SCHIP to private coverage. Under the model's base case, CBO estimates that about 23 percent of nonelderly people who are eligible for Medicaid or SCHIP have ESI coverage and that 2 percent have nongroup coverage. Some of those people might be unaware of their eligibility, but clearly some of them choose to pay for private coverage.

Take-up of private coverage mirrors take-up as described above for the formerly uninsured, although it is reduced by one-quarter in the case of ESI and reduced somewhat more in the case of nongroup coverage to reflect the lower relative plan values compared with Medicaid or SCHIP coverage. The model treats take-up of private coverage by people who lose Medicaid or SCHIP coverage (for example, because of tightening eligibility) as similar to take-up for people who chose nongroup coverage after their employers withdraw coverage. Again, take-up is a function of health status and of the cost of the private premium, which is either the employee's ESI premium (if that coverage is available) or the nongroup premium, whichever is less expensive.

CBO's model also produces a very small degree of take-up of ESI or nongroup coverage, even with no changes in relative prices, by people who are uninsured and eligible for Medicaid or SCHIP but who subsequently lose that eligibility. That take-up is based on the idea that some individuals are aware of their (or their dependents') eligibility for public coverage and believe they can enroll when they incur health care costs. That is, they would use Medicaid or SCHIP as backup insurance but would be induced to purchase private coverage if that possibility was removed.

After all changes to coverage and premiums are simulated, subsidy costs and changes in federal tax revenue can be calculated. Changes are modeled as though they occur instantaneously, but the model also allows the effects of policy changes to be phased in over the 10-year budget period.

## End Notes

[1] M. Susan Marquis and others, "Subsidies and the Demand for Individual Health Insurance in California," *Health Services Research,* vol. 39, no. 5 (2004), pp. 1547–1570; M. Susan Marquis and Stephen H. Long, "Worker Demand for Health Insurance in the Non-Group Market," *Journal of Health Economics,* vol. 14, no. 1 (1995), pp. 47–63; and Congressional Budget Office, *The Price Sensitivity of Demand for Nongroup Health Insurance.*

[2] Responsiveness at the lower end of the reported range was demonstrated by Congressional Budget Office, *The Price Sensitivity of Demand for Nongroup Insurance,* and Marquis and others, "Subsidies and the Demand for Individual Health Insurance in California." Other work has estimated responses to subsidies that were nonlinear in the subsidy level and at the high end of the range reported here. See Marquis and Long, "Worker Demand for Health Insurance in the Non-Group Market."

[3] This effect is noted in several of the studies cited above and described in the aggregate by Michael Chernew, Kevin Frick, and Catherine McLaughlin in "The Demand for Health Insurance Coverage by Low-Income Workers: Can Reduced Premiums Achieve Full Coverage?" *Health Services Research,* vol. 32, no. 4 (1997), pp. 453–470. They report that when premiums rise relative to income, the rate of uninsurance also rises, even if having health insurance becomes more valuable. They explain that result as partly attributable to the availability of free or charity care, which makes the uninsured more averse to buying insurance as premium costs rise.

[4] Jonathan Gruber and James Poterba, "Tax Incentives and the Decision to Purchase Health Insurance: Evidence from the Self-Employed," *Quarterly Journal of Economics,* vol. 109, no. 3 (1994), pp. 701–733.

[5] The quadratic form is supported in work by Linda J. Blumberg, Jessica Banthin, and Len Nichols, "Worker Decisions to Purchase Health Insurance," *Journal of Health Care Finance and Economics,* vol. 1, nos. 3–4 (2001), pp. 305–325; and by Chernew, Frick, and McLaughlin, "The Demand for Health Insurance Coverage by Low-Income Workers." Both groups presented significant coefficients on squared premiums when specifying premiums as quadratic functions.

[6] Jonathan Gruber and Ebonya Washington, "Subsidies to Employee Health Insurance Premiums and the Health Insurance Market," *Journal of Health Economics,* vol. 24, no. 2 (2005), pp. 253– 276; Blumberg, Banthin, and Nichols, "Worker Decisions to Purchase Health Insurance"; Anne Beeson Royalty and John Hagens, "The Effect of Premiums on the Decision to Participate in Health Insurance and Other Fringe Benefits Offered by the Employer: Evidence from a Real-World Experiment," *Journal of Health Economics,* vol. 24, no. 1 (2005), pp. 95–112; Chernew, Frick, and McLaughlin, "The Demand for Health Insurance Coverage by Low-Income Workers"; Thomas C. Buchmueller and Sabina Ohri, *Health Insurance Take-Up by the Near Elderly,* NBER Working Paper 11951 (Cambridge, Mass.: National Bureau of Economic Research, January 2006), www.nber.org/papers/W11951.

In: A Health Insurance Model for Analyzing... ISBN: 978-1-60741-052-2
Editor: Alan S. Burley 

*Chapter 12*

# APPLICATIONS OF THE MODEL

*Congressional Budget Office*

CBO's health insurance model is designed to examine the effects of a host of alternatives for expanding insurance coverage, including direct subsidies to individuals, removal or redistribution of current-law tax incentives, and insurance market reforms. Those options can be examined for their effects on the number of insured and uninsured people; on health expenditures; and on distributional outcomes, such as changes in insured status by age, income, and health status. The model also can be used to facilitate estimation of the federal budgetary consequences of proposals.

CBO has already used its microsimulation model to analyze proposals that would make small- and large-scale changes to the health care system. One smaller-scale option would provide a limited subsidy to low-income people to purchase private health insurance. CBO analyzed the likely consequences of such a proposal in its 2007 *Budget Options* volume. (See Appendix B for a description of that analysis.) Some policymakers also envision larger-scale changes in the health care system. The Administration's 2008 budget submission, for example, included such a policy that would significantly alter the favorable tax treatment of health insurance and provide financial inducements for people to purchase private coverage. (See Appendix C for a description of CBO's analysis of that proposal.)

As presented in this background paper, CBO's model is a work in progress. CBO will continue to improve and develop the model's capabilities to provide better analysis of proposals already made and new and modified ideas as they are developed and proposed by policymakers.

In: A Health Insurance Model for Analyzing... ISBN: 978-1-60741-052-2
Editor: Alan S. Burley 

*Chapter 13*

# APPENDIX A: INTERPRETING THE ELASTICITY OF DEMAND FOR HEALTH INSURANCE

*Congressional Budget Office*

The literature traditionally defines elasticity, as the percentage increase in quantity that results from a percentage increase in price, as in Equation (A-1):

$$\varepsilon = \frac{Q_2 - Q_1}{Q_1} \div \frac{P_2 - P_1}{P_1} \quad 1) \qquad \text{(A-1)}$$

where $Q$ is the quantity of a good purchased, and $P$ is the price (the subscripts refer to different periods of time or policy regimes).

That parameter cannot be used directly in the type of model developed by the Congressional Budget Office (CBO) because a percentage increase in quantity cannot be applied to a firm that initially does not offer insurance in the base case, where the initial offer rate is zero. (The same logic applies to individual take-up of insurance coverage.) To derive the likelihood of a new offer for a currently nonoffering firm, the CBO model employs a converted elasticity, called a take-up elasticity:

$$\varepsilon_t = \varepsilon \times \frac{Q_1}{1 - Q_1} \qquad \text{(A-2)}$$

where $\varepsilon$ is the literature-derived offer elasticity and $\varepsilon_t$ is the take-up elasticity. Thus, if 80 percent of firms of a given size currently offer coverage ($Q_1 = 0.8$), and if evidence suggests that a 10 percent decrease in premiums results in a 10 percent increase in offering (that is, there is an elasticity of –1), then one would expect 88 percent of firms to offer coverage after the change (solving for $Q_2$ in Equation [A-1]). The 8-percentage-point increase in the offer rate, from 80 percent to 88 percent, must come from among the 20 percent of nonoffering firms. Thus, the likelihood of a new offering from one of the 20 percent of firms that previously did not offer coverage is 40 percent (8 percent/20 percent). In this case, $\varepsilon_t$ would be 4 times the elasticity (–4 as opposed to –1) because of the 4-to-1 ratio of initially offering to initially nonoffering firms. Take-up rates are capped at 100 percent.

In: A Health Insurance Model for Analyzing... ISBN: 978-1-60741-052-2
Editor: Alan S. Burley 

*Chapter 14*

# APPENDIX B: ESTIMATING THE EFFECTS OF AN OPTION TO PROVIDE LOW-INCOME PEOPLE WITH A SUBSIDY TO PURCHASE HEALTH INSURANCE

***Congressional Budget Office***

The 2007 *Budget Options* volume published by the Congressional Budget Office (CBO) included an option to expand health insurance coverage by subsidizing the purchase of health insurance in the nongroup market. Under that option, the federal government would give low-income people a cash voucher or subsidy of up to $1,000 (individual) or $2,750 (family) that could be applied to the purchase of nongroup health insurance.[1] The voucher could pay as much as 90 percent of the premium and would be available to people whose household income was at or below 200 percent of the federal poverty line (the subsidy would phase out between 200 percent and 250 percent of the federal poverty line).

Using the model described in this paper, CBO estimated that such a voucher for non-group insurance coverage would result in a net decline in the uninsured population of approximately 2 million people (see Table B-1). Roughly 2.2 million of the otherwise uninsured would take up nongroup coverage because of the new subsidy. That reduction in the uninsured population would be offset somewhat because some employers that otherwise would have offered insurance to their employees would not do so if subsidized coverage were available in the nongroup market; the employers would offer higher cash wages instead. CBO estimates that roughly 900,000 people would lose access to employer-sponsored insurance (ESI) for that reason. Many of them would take up coverage in the nongroup market, and about 200,000 would lose ESI and become newly uninsured. Overall, the number of people enrolled in nongroup insurance plans would rise by more than 4 million, and the number covered by ESI would fall by a little less than 2 million. Enrollment in Medicaid or the State Children's Health Insurance Program (SCHIP) also would fall, as some 400,000 Medicaid and SCHIP beneficiaries would take up nongroup coverage instead.

The direct federal cost in the form of outlays for the vouchers would be $5.4 billion. About 60 percent of that amount would be used to subsidize insurance coverage for people who would have had coverage even without the subsidy. There also would be a federal revenue gain of $2.5 billion; the reduction in the number of employees taking up ESI would cause employers to spend less on tax-excluded health benefits and more on taxable wages. Federal outlays for Medicaid and SCHIP would fall by about $800 million because some people who otherwise would be enrolled in those programs would enroll in subsidized nongroup coverage.

CBO's estimate is similar to estimates prepared by other organizations for roughly the same proposal. One 2004 study, for example, showed an estimate of the Administration's 2004 budget proposal (which was similar to the proposal examined here) that would result in 3.1 million otherwise uninsured people taking up nongroup coverage.[2] Another organization's estimate of essentially the same proposal showed a net decrease of 3.8 million people in the ranks of the uninsured.[3] Finally, the Administration's own estimates of the 2004 proposal contained a forecast of a net reduction in the uninsured of roughly 4 million people. Although all of those estimates are higher than CBO's estimate, each involved a subsidy of the same dollar value with lower nongroup premiums (because the estimates were done several years ago) and, thus, a larger percentage subsidy. Those estimates also preceded two reports that suggested a lower response among uninsured individuals to nongroup subsidies than earlier studies had suggested.[4]

An alternative to offering a voucher for nongroup insurance would be to provide a voucher for the purchase of ESI. In that case, CBO estimates, many workers, especially those employed in small businesses, would begin to be offered insurance. If the amount of the subsidy and the income cutoffs matched those described above for nongroup insurance, about 2.4 million people (employees and their family members) would gain access to ESI (see

Table B-1). The number of uninsured people would decline by 2 million, with some people taking up coverage under those new offers of ESI and some taking up coverage under offers they had previously declined but that would now be eligible for the new subsidy. The number of people covered by ESI would increase by 3 million; nongroup insurance would cover about 100,000 fewer people. The subsidy would induce about 900,000 Medicaid and SCHIP enrollees to switch to ESI coverage.

**Table B-1. Effects of Subsidy for Health Insurance, 2008**

| | Base Case | Change Under a Subsidy for Nongroup Insurance | Change Under a Subsidy for ESI |
|---|---|---|---|
| **Impact on Health Insurance Status of U.S. Nonelderly Population (Millions)** | | | |
| People with Access to ESI Offer | 185.8 | -0.9 | 2.4 |
| Uninsured | 44.2 | -2.0 | -2.0 |
| Uninsured to nongroup | n.a. | 2.2 | * |
| Uninsured to ESI | n.a. | * | 2.0 |
| ESI to uninsured | n.a. | 0.2 | * |
| Insured | | | |
| ESI | 161.4 | -1.8 | 3.0 |
| Nongroup | 10.2 | 4.3 | -0.1 |
| Medicaid and SCHIP | 42.1 | -0.4 | -0.9 |
| **Impact on Federal Budget (Billions of dollars)** | | | |
| Subsidy Cost | n.a. | 5.4 | 23.6 |
| Cost for previously uninsured | n.a. | 2.0 | 1.6 |
| Revenue Gain | n.a. | 2.5 | 4.0 |
| Savings in Medicaid and SCHIP | n.a. | 0.8 | 1.8 |
| Net Cost | n.a. | 2.1 | 17.8 |

Source: Congressional Budget Office's health insurance simulation model.

Note: ESI = employer-sponsored insurance; n.a. = not applicable; * = population change of fewer than 500,000 people; SCHIP = State Children's Health Insurance Program.

Less than 10 percent of the subsidy outlay in the ESI scenario would be provided to otherwise uninsured individuals, compared with about 40 percent in the case of the nongroup subsidy. The implication is that the cost per newly insured person would be higher in the case of an ESI subsidy than it would be for a nongroup subsidy. Non-group insurance, however, might be inferior to ESI because it costs more per dollar of insured benefit (because of higher administrative costs) and may place limits on coverage.

## End Notes

[1] See Congressional Budget Office, *Budget Options* (February 2007), Option 550-11, p. 158.

[2] Henry J. Kaiser Family Foundation, *Coverage and Cost Impacts of the President's Health Insurance Tax Credit and Tax Deduction Proposals,* Issue Brief 7049 (Washington, D.C.: Henry J. Kaiser Family Foundation, March 2004), available from www.kff.org/insurance/7049.cfm.

[3] See Sherry Glied and Douglas Gould, "Variations in the Impact of Health Coverage Expansion Proposals Across States," *Health Affairs,* Web Exclusive, W5-270 (June 7, 2005), http://content.healthaffairs.org/cgi/content/full/hlthaff.w5.259/DC1.

[4] See Congressional Budget Office, *The Price Sensitivity of Demand for Nongroup Health Insurance* (August 2005); and M. Susan Marquis and others, "Subsidies and the Demand for Individual Health Insurance in California," *Health Services Research,* vol. 39, no. 5 (2004), pp. 1547–1570.

In: A Health Insurance Model for Analyzing... ISBN: 978-1-60741-052-2
Editor: Alan S. Burley 

*Chapter 15*

# APPENDIX C: ESTIMATING THE EFFECTS OF THE ADMINISTRATION'S 2008 HEALTH INSURANCE BUDGET PROPOSAL

***Congressional Budget Office***

The President's 2008 budget request proposed to replace virtually all of the current tax preferences for health insurance with a new standard deduction for any taxpayer who buys a qualifying health insurance plan. The Congressional Budget Office (CBO) used its health insurance microsimulation model to calculate the effects that proposal would have on the number of uninsured and other relevant outcomes.[1]

To qualify for the tax deduction, a health insurance plan would have to meet requirements that include a specific limit on out-of-pocket expenses, caps on annual or lifetime benefits, adherence to rules about the types of care covered, and guaranteed renewability.[2] Nearly all current health plans would be expected to qualify, although some policies sold in the individual insurance market might not meet those standards. Taxpayers who bought qualifying health plans—whether through an employer or independently—would receive a deduction against their earnings (for income and payroll tax purposes) of $15,000 for family coverage and $7,500 for single coverage (in 2008 dollars).

CBO estimated that the President's health proposal would reduce the number of uninsured people by about 6.7 million in 2010, assuming the market had fully adjusted to the change in the law (see Table C-1). The overall reduction in the number of uninsured individuals reflects many channels of change in the health insurance market. Of people who would otherwise be uninsured, for example, an estimated 7 million would become insured in the nongroup market under the proposal, and about 1.3 million would obtain employer-sponsored insurance (ESI). At the same time, about 1.5 million people who would have ESI in 2010 under current law would become uninsured under the proposal, and about 6.3 million would switch from ESI to nongroup coverage.

The amount of the proposed tax deduction would represent a subsidy of about 70 percent of the health insurance premiums for the average person who became newly insured through the nongroup market. That subsidy rate would vary among individuals and households depending on factors such as taxable income, the type and comprehensiveness of the insurance purchased, and the taxpayer's age and health status (which could affect quoted premiums).

Compared with people who would be uninsured in 2010 under current law, those gaining insurance coverage under the President's proposal would have higher income, on average. The reason is that the value of the new deduction would be greater for people with higher marginal tax rates, which are associated with higher incomes. Nonetheless, most newly insured people would come from lower-middle- and middle-income households, mostly because the uninsured population as a group has relatively low income compared with the population as a whole. The uninsured people who would acquire insurance coverage under the proposal would also have better health status, on average, than the uninsured population at large because premiums in the nongroup market are generally lower for people with lower expected health costs, so the proposed deduction would represent a larger percentage subsidy of premiums for people with lower expected costs.

Replacing the current tax exclusion for ESI plans with a deduction that could be used in either the ESI or the nongroup market, as in the President's proposal, would make ESI plans less attractive relative to nongroup plans than they are now.[3] As a result, CBO estimates that the number of people with ESI would decline by more than 6 million. The bulk of the people losing coverage in the ESI market would obtain insurance through the nongroup market, although some would become uninsured.

Despite the significant change in tax treatment, the vast majority of privately insured individuals would remain in the ESI market rather than the nongroup market, because the former has significantly lower administrative costs and advantages in forming insurance pools with more predictable costs. Nevertheless, the number of people obtaining coverage through the nongroup market would increase significantly, mainly as a result of newly insured individuals and those who would switch from ESI to nongroup coverage.

The change from the current system, in which the tax exclusion creates a larger tax subsidy for higher expenditures on health insurance, to a fixed deduction that is independent of the comprehensiveness of a health plan would cause people to buy plans with less generous benefits (that is, plans with lower relative plan value), on average. CBO estimates that the extent of that benefit reduction—combining both the effects of people purchasing ESI plans with less generous benefits and a shift in coverage toward the nongroup market (where coverage is typically less generous)—would amount to roughly 15 percent in 2010.

**Table C-1. Effects of the Administration's 2008 Budget Proposal, 2010**

| | Base Case | Administration's Proposal |
|---|---|---|
| **Impact on Health Insurance Status of U.S. Nonelderly Population (Millions)** | | |
| People with Access to ESI Offer | 187.1 | -8.7 |
| Uninsured | 45.7 | -6.7 |
| Uninsured to nongroup | n.a. | 7.0 |
| Uninsured to ESI | n.a. | 1.3 |
| ESI to uninsured | n.a. | 1.5 |
| Insured | | |
| ESI | 162.5 | -6.6 |
| Nongroup | 10.3 | 13.6 |
| Medicaid and SCHIP | 43.2 | -0.5 |
| **Impact on Federal Budget (Billions of dollars)[a]** | | |
| Subsidy Cost | n.a. | 323.2 |
| Miscellaneous Costs | n.a. | 6.5 |
| Revenue Gain | n.a. | 312.8 |
| Net Cost[a] | n.a. | 16.9 |

Source: Congressional Budget Office's health insurance simulation model.

Note: ESI = employer-sponsored insurance; n.a. = not applicable; SCHIP = State Children's Health Insurance Program.

a. Data on the impact on the federal budget come from Joint Committee on Taxation, *Estimating the Revenue Effects of the President's Fiscal Year 2008 Poposal Providing a Standard Deduction for Health Insurance: Modeling and Assumptions* (March 20, 2007), Table 1, p. 20.

## End Notes

[1] See Congressional Budget Office, *An Analysis of the President's Budgetary Proposals for Fiscal Year 2008* (March 2007).

[2] The limits on out-of-pocket costs would be based on the standards that apply to health savings account plans; currently, those limits cannot exceed $5,500 for individuals and $11,000 for family policies (amounts that are indexed to increase with overall inflation). Other requirements for the new deduction would be established by the Treasury Department through regulation. Those rules would not preempt states' minimum standards for health insurance coverage.

[3] Under current law, self-employed people can take an income tax deduction for health insurance premiums even though they often purchase insurance through the traditional nongroup market.

# SELECTED BIBLIOGRAPHY

Actuarial Research Corporation, *Study of the Administrative Costs and Actuarial Values of Small Health Plans* (prepared for the Small Business Administration Office of Advocacy, January 2003).

AHIP Center for Policy and Research, *Individual Health Insurance: A Comprehensive Survey of Affordability, Access, and Benefits.* (Washington, D.C.: America's Health Insurance Plans, August 2005), www.ahipresearch.org/bytopic.html.

Anne Beeson Royalty & John Hagens (2005). "The Effect of Premiums on the Decision to Participate in Health Insurance and Other Fringe Benefits Offered by the Employer: Evidence from a Real-World Experiment," *Journal of Health Economics, vol. 24, no. 1*, pp. 95–112.

Commonwealth of Massachusetts, "*Connector Board Endorses Plans from Seven Carriers*" (press release issued by the Commonwealth Health Insurance Connector Authority, March 8, 2007).

Congressional Budget Office, *The Price Sensitivity of Demand for Nongroup Health Insurance* (August 2005), www.cbo.gov/publications.

Catherine Hoffman and John Holahan, *What Is the Current Population Survey Telling Us About the Number of Uninsured?* Issue Paper, Kaiser Commission on Medicaid and the Uninsured (Menlo Park, Calif.: Henry J. Kaiser Family Foundation, August 2005), www.kff.org/uninsured/upload/7384.pdf.

Daniel Feenberg & Elisabeth Coutts, (1993). "An Introduction to the TAXSIM Model," *Journal of Policy Analysis and Management, vol. 12, no. 1*, pp. 189–194, www.nber.org/~taxsim/feenberg-coutts.pdf.

General Accounting Office, *Health Insurance Regulation: Varying State Requirements Affect Cost of Insurance,* GAO/HEHS-96-161 (August 1996), www.gao.gov/ archive/1996/he96161.pdf.

Henry, J. (2004). Kaiser Family Foundation, *Coverage and Cost Impacts of the President's Health Insurance Tax Credit and Tax Deduction Proposals,* Issue Brief 7049 (Menlo Park, Calif.: Henry J. Kaiser Family Foundation, March), available from www.kff.org/insurance/7049.cfm.

Henry J. (2004). Kaiser Family Foundation, *Employer Health Benefits 2004 Annual Survey* (Menlo Park, Calif.: Henry J. Kaiser Family Foundation and Health Research and Education Trust, September), Exhibit 2.3, p. 38, available from www.kff.org/insurance/7148/index.cfm.

Jonathan Gruber & Michael Lettau. (2004). "How Elastic Is the Firm's Demand for Health Insurance?" *Journal of Public Economics, vol. 88, nos. 7–8,* pp. 1273–1293.

Jonathan Gruber & Robin McKnight. (2003) "Why Did Employee Health Insurance Contributions Rise?" *Journal of Health Economics, vol. 22, no. 6,* pp. 1085–1104.

Jonathan Gruber & James Poterba. (1994)."Tax Incentives and the Decision to Purchase Health Insurance: Evidence from the Self-Employed," *Quarterly Journal of Economics, vol. 109, no. 3,* pp. 701–733.

Jonathan Gruber & Ebonya Washington. (2005). "Subsidies to Employee Health Insurance Premiums and the Health Insurance Market," *Journal of Health Economics, vol. 24, no. 2*, pp. 253–276.

Jack Hadley & John Holahan. (2003). *Who Pays and How Much? The Cost of Caring for the Uninsured* (Washington, D.C.: Urban Institute, February), www.kff.org/uninsured/loader.cfm?url=/commonspot/security/getfile.cfm &PageID=14319.

Jack Hadley & James, D. (2002). Reschovsky, "Small Firms' Demand for Health Insurance: The Decision to Offer Insurance," *Inquiry, vol. 39, no. 2*, pp. 118–137.

Jon Gabel & others. (2007). "Trends in the Golden State: Small-Group Premiums Rise Sharply While Actuarial Values for Individual Coverage Plummet," *Health Affairs, Web exclusive, vol. 26, no. 4*, w488–w499.

John Sheils & Randall Haught. (2003). *Covering America: Cost and Coverage Analysis of Ten Proposals to Expand Health Insurance Coverage* (Falls Church, Va.: Lewin Group, October), available from www.lewin.com/NewsEvents/Publications.

Linda, J. Blumberg, Jessica Banthin & Len Nichols. (2001). "Worker Decisions to Purchase Health Insurance," *Journal of Health Care Finance and Economics, vol. 1, nos. 3–4,* pp. 305–325.

Len Nichols & Linda, J. (1999). *Blumberg, "Estimating Employer Elasticity of Demand for Health Insurance"* (paper presented at Academy Health Annual Research Meeting, Washington, D.C.,).

Melinda Beeuwkes Buntin, M. Susan Marquis, & Jill M. (2004). Yegian, "The Role of the Individual Health Insurance Market and Prospects for Change," *Health Affairs, vol. 23, no. 6,* pp. 79–90, http://content.healthaffairs.org/cgi/content/full/ 23/6/79.

Michael Chernew, David, M. Cutler & Patricia Seliger. (2005). Keenan, "Increasing Health Insurance Costs and the Decline in Insurance Coverage," *Health Services Research, vol. 40, no. 4* pp. 1021–1039, www.blackwell-synergy.com/doi/pdf/10.1111/j.1475-6773.2005.00409.x?cookieSet=1.

Michael Chernew, Kevin Frick & Catherine McLaughlin. (1997). "The Demand for Health Insurance Coverage by Low-Income Workers: Can Reduced Premiums Achieve Full Coverage?" *Health Services Research, vol. 32, no. 4,* pp. 453–470.

Michael Davern, Jacob Alex Klerman, & Jeanette Ziegenfuss. (2007). *Medicaid Under-Reporting in the Current Population Survey and One Approach for a Partial Correction* (Minneapolis, Minnesota: University of Minnesota State Health Access Data Assistance Center, October 15,), http://cps.ipums.org/cps/medadjust.pdf.

Mark Merlis. (2005). *Fundamentals of Underwriting in the Nongroup Health Insurance Market: Access to Coverage and Options for Reform,* National Health Policy Forum Background Paper (Washington, D.C.: George Washington University, April), www.nhpf.org/pdfs_bp/BP_Underwriting_04-13-05.pdf.

Mark Pauly. (2007). "The Demand for Health Insurance in the Group Setting: Can You Always Get What You Want?" *Journal of Risk & Insurance, vol. 74, no. 1,* pp. 115–140.

Richard Kronick & Todd Gilmer. (1999). "Explaining the Decline in Health Insurance Coverage: 1979–1995," *Health Affairs, vol. 18, no. 2,* pp. 30–47.

Sherry Glied & Douglas Gould. (2005). "Variations in the Impact of Health Coverage Expansion Proposals Across States," *Health Affairs,* Web Exclusive, W5-270, June 7, http://content.healthaffairs.org/cgi/content/full/hlthaff.w5.259/DC1.

Sherry Glied & Sarah Little. (2003). "*The Price of Health Insurance: Modeling Premiums in Models of Insurance Expansions*" (paper presented at an Academy Health conference, "Determinants of Premiums in the Individual Market," Washington, D.C., November 12,).

Sherry Glied & Joshua Graff Zivin. (2004). *Modeling Employer Decisions to Offer Health Insurance,* Robert Wood Johnson Foundation Working Paper (Princeton, N.J.: Robert Wood Johnson Foundation, revised August), www.rwjf.org/pr/synthesis/reports_and_briefs/pdf/no7_researchabstract.pdf.

Susan Marquis, M. & Stephen H. (1995). Long, "Worker Demand for Health Insurance in the Non-Group Market," *Journal of Health Economics, vol. 14, no. 1,* pp. 47–63.

Susan Marquis, M. & others. (2004). "Subsidies and the Demand for Individual Health Insurance in California," *Health Services Research, vol. 39, no. 5,* pp. 1547–1570.

Thomas, C. Buchmueller & others. (2005). "The Effect of SCHIP Expansions on Health Insurance Decisions by Employers," *Inquiry, vol. 42, no. 3,* pp. 218–231.

Thomas, C. (2006). Buchmueller and Sabina Ohri, *Health Insurance Take-Up by the Near Elderly,* NBER Working Paper 11951 (Cambridge, Mass.: National Bureau of Economic Research, January), www.nber.org/papers/W11951.

# INDEX

## R



## S



## T

## U



## V



## W